D1119181

$\mathcal{C}$ongratulations for taking on the important responsibility of family photo historian – you know the value of organizing and preserving the photos and stories of your life.

Creative Memories originated the photo preservation Home Class and Workshop program in 1987. In those ten years we have learned that scrapbook page layout ideas and styles vary from the simple to the elaborate. We have also learned that creative inspiration, no matter what your style, does not always come when it is needed. This book is filled with exclusive page designs and photo layout ideas to stimulate your creativity and keep your projects moving forward.

You may choose to recreate an entire page design or simply a small portion. You will want to check with your Creative Memories Consultant about the current availability of the sticker and die cut shapes featured. If something is not available, we invite you to make your own creative substitutions.

We proudly acknowledge the many Creative Memories Consultants in the United States and Canada who designed pages for this book – their names are printed along side their layout.

May your albums be a continuous celebration of your life!

CREATIVE MEMORIES

a decade of preserving lifetimes

Table of Contents

Holidays

Miscellaneous Theme

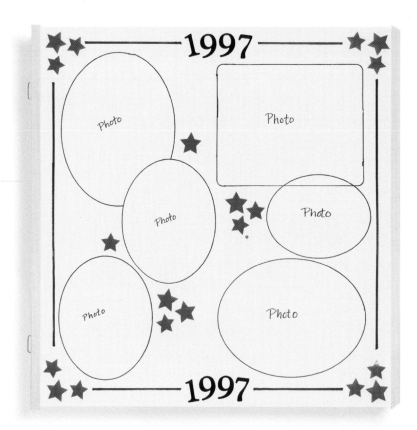

Materials:
- Creative Memories Black 123 Stickers
- Gold Star Stickers (Special Occasion Pack)
- Black Calligraphy Pen
- Oval Template

Consultant: Lynnette Adams
State: Washington

Materials:
- Creative Memories Black ABC Stickers
- Musical Instrument Stickers (Big Pack)
- Bear Sticker (Decorative Pack)
- Black Music Notes, Top Hat with Rose & Bow Tie Stickers (Special Occasion Pack)
- Black Photo Mounting Paper (Contemporary Pack)
- Cranberry & Cranberry Gingham Photo Mounting Paper
- Creative Memories Borderlines™ – *Wavy*
- Corner Rounder

Special Instructions:
- Create border using wavy Borderlines™ and photo mounting paper

Consultant: Kimberly Arens
State: Nebraska

NEW YEAR

Materials:
- Creative Memories Sky Blue ABC Stickers
- Party Hats & Confetti Stickers (Decorative Pack)
- Sky Blue, Raspberry, Purple and Hot Pink Photo Mounting Paper (Contemporary Pack)
- Pink Fine-Tip Pen
- Circle Cutter
- Oval Template

Special Instructions:
- Draw and cut clock stem out of photo mounting paper

Consultant: Vicki Albu
State: Minnesota

VALENTINE'S DAY

Materials:
- Cinnamon Heart & Ivy Stickers (Special Occasion Pack)
- Die Cut Cupid
- Heart Template
- Red Photo Mounting Paper (Contemporary Pack)
- Cranberry Gingham Photo Mounting Paper
- Black Fine-Tip Pen
- Red Calligraphy Pen
- Creative Memories Borderlines™ – *Wavy*

Special Instructions:
- Trace wavy Borderlines™ with red calligraphy pen to create ribbon

Combined Ideas From:
Consultant: Beth Bassett
State: Florida
Consultant: Janice Bacich
Designed by: Customer
Jill Swogger
State: Pennsylvania

Materials:
- Musical Instrument Stickers (Big Pack)
- Micro Music Note Stickers (Decorative Pack)
- Die Cut Heart
- Black Fine-Tip, Calligraphy Pens
- Creative Memories Borderlines™ – *Wavy*

Consultant: Judy Bailey
State: Texas

VALENTINE'S DAY

Materials:
- Creative Memories Red ABC Stickers
- Cinnamon Hearts, Top Hats with Rose & Bow Tie Stickers (Special Occasion Pack)
- Red Calligraphy Pen
- Creative Memories Borderlines™ – *Victorian*

Consultant: Diane Noel
State: Florida

Materials:
- Creative Memories Sky Blue & Raspberry ABC/123 Stickers
- Flowers, Bows & Confetti Stickers (Creative Memories Introductory Pack)
- Multi Bows (Decorative Pack)
- Die Cut Cowboy Hat, Basket & Floppy Eared Bunny
- Black Fine-Tip Pen
- Yellow Sumi Brush Pen

Special Instructions:
- Overlap ABC/123 Stickers
- Color in facial features of Floppy Eared Bunny with black fine-tip pen
- Color in weave lines of basket with Yellow Sumi Brush pen

Consultant: Sheila Bolka
State: California

Materials:
- Creative Memories Lilac ABC Stickers
- Easter Bunny & Easter Egg Stickers (Special Occasion Pack)
- Grass Stickers (Decorative Pack)
- Oval Template

Consultant: Christine Boykin
State: Ohio

Materials:
- Creative Memories Black ABC Stickers
- Ivy Stickers (Special Occasion Pack)
- Die Cut Cross
- Sky Blue Photo Mounting Paper (Contemporary Pack)
- White Photo Mounting Paper
- Circle Template or Circle Cutter

Consultant: Sheila Bolka
State: California

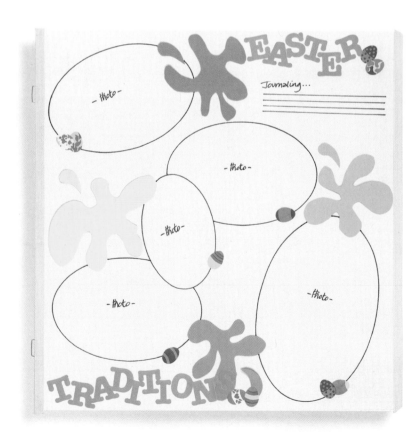

Materials:
- Creative Memories Light Pink ABC Stickers
- Egg Stickers (Special Occasion Pack)
- Yellow, Lilac, Light Pink and Light Blue Photo Mounting Paper (Contemporary Pack)
- Black Fine-Tip Pen
- Oval Template

Special Instructions
- Draw and cut out "splashes" on photo mounting paper
- Use fine-tip pen for journaling

Consultant: Narda Poe
State: Texas

Materials:
- Cinnamon Hearts, Christmas Bow, Ivy & Small Rose Stickers (Special Occasion Pack)
- Brown Fine-Tip Pen
- Brown Calligraphy Pen
- Scallop Heart Template

Special Instructions:
- Trace heart template and arrange with ivy and cinnamon hearts

Consultant: Cheryl Calvert
State: Montana

Materials:
- Quilted Hearts, Micro Hearts & Multi Bows Stickers (Decorative Pack)
- Die Cut Scallop Heart
- Fine-Tip Pen Set
- Calligraphy Pen Set
- Creative Memories Borderlines™ – *Victorian*
- Circle & Oval Templates
- Corner Rounder

Consultant: Leslie Buckley
State: Mississippi

Materials:
- Creative Memories Black ABC Stickers
- Tool Stickers (Decorative Pack)
- Die Cut Saw & Hammers
- Black Calligraphy Pen
- Creative Memories Borderlines™ – *Scallop*
- Red, Gold & Sky Blue Photo Mounting Paper (Contemporary Pack)

Consultant: Carmen Frey
State: California

Materials:
- Creative Memories Blue & Red ABC/123 Stickers
- Gold Star Stickers (Decorative Pack)
- Red & Blue Star Stickers (Creative Memories Introductory Pack)
- Die Cut Firecrackers

Special Instructions:
- Overlap Blue & Red ABC/123 Stickers

Consultant: Leslie Clark
State: Utah

Materials:
- Creative Memories Black ABC Stickers
- Graduation, Silver & Gold Confetti Stickers (Special Occasion Pack)
- Die Cut Number Stencils
- Evergreen & Deep Blue Photo Mounting Paper
- Black Calligraphy Pen

Special Instructions:
- Trace die cut number stencils with Black Calligraphy Pen
- Draw and cut pieces of graduation cap from photo mounting paper

Consultant: Amy Cordon
State: Utah

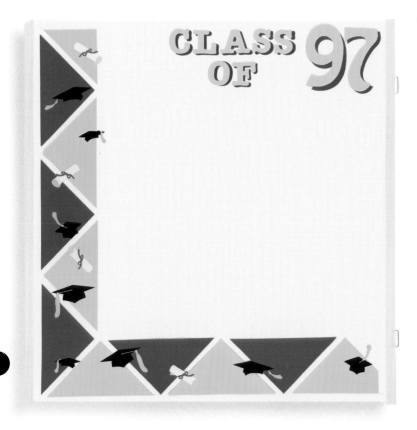

Materials:
- Creative Memories Gold & Blue ABC Stickers
- Graduation Stickers (Special Occasion Pack)
- Die Cut Numbers
- Gold & Nautical Blue Photo Mounting Paper (Contemporary Pack)

Special Instructions:
- Overlap Gold & Blue ABC Stickers and die cut numbers
- Cut 2¹/₂ inch squares of photo mounting paper, then cut in half to make triangles

Note: You can change the color scheme to your school colors

Consultant: Susan Coons
State: Georgia

GRADUATION

Materials:
- Creative Memories Black ABC Stickers
- Graduation & Flag Stickers (Special Occasion Pack)
- Die Cut Miniature Apple
- Creative Memories Borderlines™ - *Victorian*
- Red Fine-Tip Pen

Consultant: Laurie Monfreda
State: Vermont

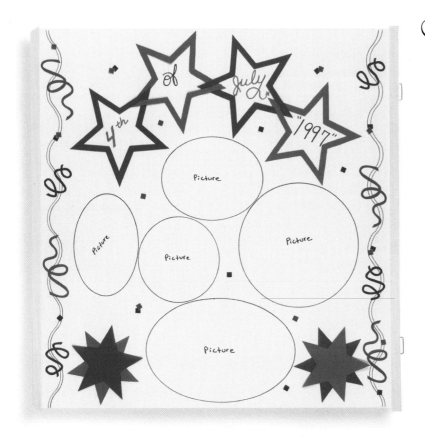

FOURTH OF JULY

Materials:
- Confetti Stickers (Creative Memories Introductory Pack)
- Die Cut Stars
- Blue & Red Fine-Tip Pens
- Creative Memories Borderlines™ – *Wavy*
- Circle & Oval Templates

Special Instructions:
- Cut through die-cut stars to weave together

Consultant: Ann Marie Donovan
State: Massachusetts

Materials:
- Cranberry, White & Deep Blue Photo Mounting Paper
- Blue Calligraphy Pen
- Star Template
- Oval Template

Consultant: Shelley Dodson
State: Arizona

Materials:
- Creative Memories Black ABC/123 Stickers
- Confetti Stickers (Creative Memories Introductory Pack)
- Flags & Music Note Stickers (Special Occasion Pack)
- Black Fine-Tip Pen

Consultant: Janet Distelzweig
State: Michigan

Special Instructions:
• Draw and cut dynamite sticks and wicks from Navy Blue Photo Mounting Paper

Consultant: Melodie D. DeArmond
State: Florida

Materials:
• Red & Navy Blue Photo Mounting Paper (Classic Pack)
• White Photo Mounting Paper
• Star Template
• Creative Memories Borderlines™ – *Wavy*
• Corner Rounder

$\mathscr{D}$OUBLE PAGE SPREAD

Materials:
- Creative Memories Black ABC Stickers
- Halloween Candy, Trick or Treaters & Pumpkin Stickers (Special Occasion Pack)
- Black & Orange Fine-Tip Pens

Customer: Christen J. S. Cahoon
State: Texas

HALLOWEEN

Materials:
- Halloween Candy & Trick or Treater Stickers (Special Occasion Pack)
- Candy Stickers (Decorative Pack)
- Die Cut Letters
- Die Cut Pumpkin
- Green & Black Photo Mounting Paper (Contemporary Pack)
- Black Fine-Tip Pen

Special Instructions:
- Draw and cut ghost and bat out of photo mounting paper
- Draw face on pumpkin

Consultant: Sonya Eastland
State: Missouri

Materials:
- Halloween Candy, Pumpkin & Trick or Treater Stickers (Special Occasion Pack)
- Circle Template
- Black Fine-Tip Pen

Special Instructions:
- Trace four circles on the page
- Place a Trick or Treater in each circle
- Cut the tops off of the pumpkin stickers, then place on top of the Trick or Treater Stickers

Consultant: Lisa Thurman
State: Virginia

HALLOWEEN

Materials:
- Creative Memories Black ABC Stickers
- Pumpkin & Ivy Stickers (Decorative Pack)
- Die Cut Black Cat
- Gold Photo Mounting Paper (Contemporary Pack)
- Creative Memories Borderlines™ – *Scallop*
- Brown, Black & Orange Fine-Tip Pens
- Circle Cutter or Circle Template

Special Instructions:
- Decorate ABC stickers with the orange and black pens
- Using the scallop Borderlines™, draw fence top

Consultant: Vicky Funfar
State: California

Materials:
- Small Leaves & Autumn Border Stickers (Special Occasion Pack)
- Orange Fine-Tip Pen
- Black Calligraphy Pen

Consultant: Tammie Frazier
State: Colorado

Materials:
- Creative Memories Gold ABC Stickers
- Pumpkin, Small Apple & Ivy Stickers (Special Occasion Pack)
- Die Cut Turkey
- Orange Fine-Tip Pen
- Creative Memories Borderlines™ – *Wavy*

Consultant: Luana Bastien
State: California

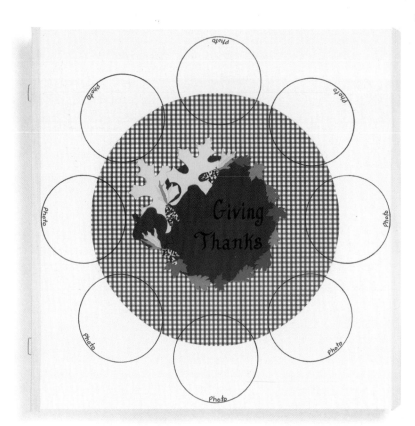

Materials:
- Small Leaves & Autumn Border Stickers (Special Occasion Pack)
- Die Cut Oak Leaves & Acorns
- Evergreen & Evergreen Gingham Photo Mounting Paper
- Black Calligraphy Pen
- Circle Cutter or Circle Template

Special Instructions:
- Use circle cutter or template to cut photographs

Consultant: Sue Fisher
State: Michigan

CHRISTMAS

Materials:
- Candy Cane Stickers (Creative Memories Introductory Pack)
- Micro Music Note Stickers (Decorative Pack)
- Die Cut Carolers
- Red Calligraphy Pen
- Black & Green Fine-Tip Pens

Combined Ideas From:
Consultant: Sheri Berger
State: Missouri
Consultant: Tina Seely
State: Oregon

Materials:
- Merry Christmas, Holly & Ornament Stickers (Creative Memories Christmas Pack)
- Candle & Gift Stickers (Creative Memories Wedding Pack)
- Green Fine-Tip Pen

Consultant: Melynna Wolk
State: Missouri

Materials:
- Ivy, Small Rose & Snow Tree Stickers (Special Occasion Pack)
- Die Cut Cathedral Window
- Evergreen, Cranberry Gingham & Evergreen Gingham Photo Mounting Paper
- Geometric Template

Consultant: Traci Goshen and Customer Julie Johnson
State: California

Materials:
- Creative Memories Black ABC Stickers
- Black Music Note, Jingle Bell and Christmas Bow Stickers (Special Occasion Pack)
- Die Cut Horse
- Cranberry Photo Mounting Paper

Special Instructions:
- Draw and cut out sleigh from cranberry photo mounting paper or see your Creative Memories Consultant for a die cut sleigh

Consultant: Carol Wang
Province: Alberta

Materials:
- Creative Memories Red ABC Stickers
- Candy Cane Stickers (Creative Memories Introductory Pack)
- Elves & Christmas Border Stickers (Special Occasion Pack)
- Toy Stickers (Decorative Pack)
- Die Cut Train & Christmas Lights
- Green Fine-Tip Pen
- Creative Memories Borderlines™ – *Wavy*

Consultant: Janice Greig
State: Minnesota

Materials:
- Christmas Bow Stickers (Special Occasion Pack)
- Die Cut Gingerbread Man
- White, Cranberry & Evergreen Photo Mounting Paper
- Creative Memories Borderlines™ – *Wavy*
- Alpine Scissors

Special Instructions:
- Cut two strips each of Cranberry and Evergreen photo mounting paper – weave together

Combined Ideas From:
Consultant: Lisa Knott
State: California
Consultant: Kristy Woodard
State: Georgia

SEASON'S GREETINGS

Materials:
- Creative Memories Cranberry & Evergreen ABC/123 Stickers
- Christmas Bow Stickers (Special Occasion Pack)
- Cranberry, Evergreen, Deep Blue, Cranberry Gingham & Evergreen Gingham Photo Mounting Paper
- Alpine Scissors
- Circle Cutter or Circle Template

Special Instructions:
- Overlap ABC/123 Stickers

Consultant: Tammy Daum and Nora Elkins
State: Florida

Special Instructions:
- Place Gingham photo mounting paper behind ornaments
- Cut edges off of the die cut stencils with Alpine Scissors

Consultant: JoAnn Gilbert
State: California

Materials:
- Christmas Stickers (Creative Memories Christmas Pack)
- Christmas Bow Stickers (Special Occasion Pack)
- Die Cut Ornaments & their Stencils
- Cranberry, Cranberry Gingham, Evergreen & Evergreen Gingham Photo Mounting Paper
- Alpine Scissors

DOUBLE PAGE SPREAD

Materials:
- Geometric & Present Stickers (Big Pack)
- Christmas Light Stickers (Special Occasion)
- Die Cut Letters
- Gold Photo Mounting Paper (Contemporary Pack)

Special Instructions:
- Make candles using geometric stickers
- Cut off Christmas lights and use for flame

Consultant: Shari Krandel
State: California

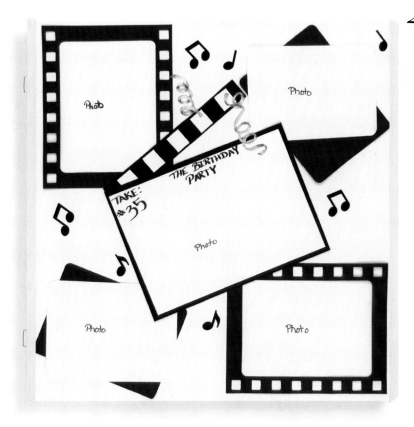

ADULT BIRTHDAY

Materials:
- Black Music Notes (Special Occasion Pack)
- Confetti Stickers (Creative Memories Wedding Pack)
- Die Cut Film Frame & Inside Square
- White Photo Mounting Paper
- Black Photo Mounting Paper (Classic Pack)
- Black Calligraphy Pen
- Corner Rounder

Special Instructions:
- Use the inside square from the die cut film frame to mount photos on

Consultant: Kim Hornbaker
State: Florida

Consultant: Michelle Houle
Province: British Columbia

Materials:

- Creative Memories Blue ABC/123 Stickers
- Super Star Strickers (Decorative Pack)
- Die Cut Numbers
- Die Cut Firecrackers
- Green, Purple, Red & Nautical Blue Photo Mounting Paper (Contemporary Pack)
- Star Template
- Circle Cutter or Circle Template

DOUBLE PAGE SPREAD

Materials:
- Creative Memories Black ABC Stickers
- Balloon and Stars & Confetti Stickers (Creative Memories Introductory Pack)

Consultant: Sheryl Ingravallo
State: California

BABY

Materials:
- Creative Memories Gold ABC Stickers
- Baby Stickers (Big Pack)
- Deep Blue Gingham Photo Mounting Paper
- Gold Photo Mounting Paper (Contemporary Pack)
- Green Calligraphy Pen
- Geometric Template

Special Instructions:
- Using the Geometric Template, cut two diamonds out of Deep Blue Gingham photo mounting paper and one out of gold photo mounting paper

Consultant: Kimberly Spurlock
State: Texas

Materials:
- Baby Stickers (Big Pack)
- Green Calligraphy Pen
- Black Fine-Tip Pen

Consultant: Vesna Grieco
State: California

BABY

Materials:
- Baby Stickers (Creative
  Memories Introductory Pack)
- Baby Stickers (Big Pack)
- Die Cut Stork
- Light Pink, Light Blue &
  Yellow Photo Mounting Paper
  (Contemporary Pack)

Consultant: Christine Boykin
State: Ohio

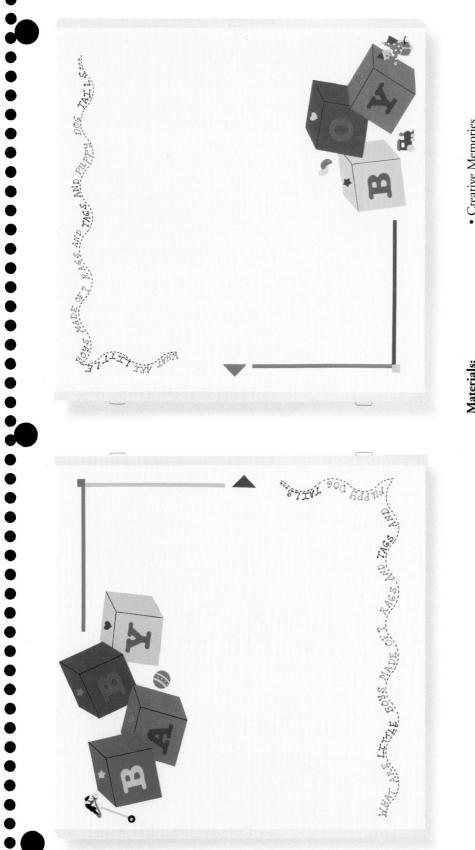

BOYS MADE OF? RAGS AND TAGS AND PUPPY DOG TAILS

WHAT ARE LITTLE

PUPPY DOG TAILS

WHAT ARE LITTLE BOYS MADE OF? RAGS AND TAGS AND

• Creative Memories
Borderlines™ – *Wavy*

Special Instructions:
• Draw and cut blocks out of photo mounting paper
• Draw dash line using the wavy Borderlines™

Consultant: Arletta J. Herman
State: Montana

Materials:
• Creative Memories Red, Gold, Green & Blue ABC Stickers
• Geometric Stickers (Big Pack)
• Toy, Candy, Micro Heart & Micro Star Stickers (Decorative Pack)
• Red, Gold, Green & Nautical Blue Photo Mounting Paper (Contemporary Pack)
• Fine-Tip Pen Set

𝒟OUBLE PAGE SPREAD

Materials:
- Creative Memories Light Blue & Yellow ABC Stickers
- Baby Stickers (Big Pack)
- Die Cut Duck & Old-Fashion Tub
- Blue Calligraphy Pen
- Creative Memories Borderlines™– *Ocean*
- Circle Cutter or Circle Template

Special Instructions:
- Cut photos with the Circle Cutter or Circle Template to represent bubbles

Consultant: Shannon Young
State: Mississippi

ℬORDERS

Materials:
- Flower & Bow Stickers (Creative Memories Introductory Pack)
- Pink Calligraphy Pen
- Green Fine-Tip Pen
- Template

Special Instructions:
- Trace the edge of a template to achieve the straight edge and round corner border

Consultant: Sheri Berger
State: Missouri

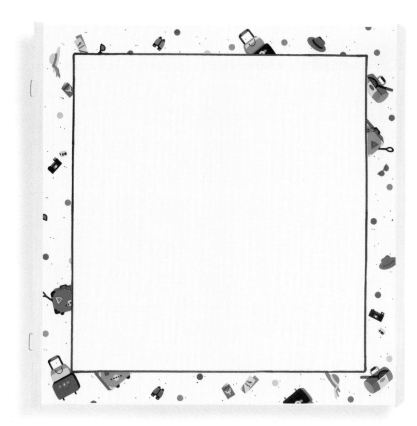

Materials:
- Party & Travel Gear Stickers (Decorative Pack)
- Black Fine-Tip & Calligraphy Pens

Consultant: Marcia Fraley
State: California

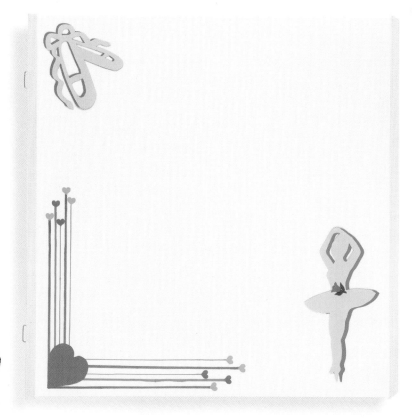

Materials:
- Flower Stickers (Creative Memories Introductory Pack)
- Micro Heart Stickers (Decorative Pack)
- Die Cut Ballerina/Slippers & Heart
- Red & Pink Fine-Tip Pen
- Red & Pink Calligraphy Pen

Combined Ideas From:
Consultants: Karyn Alba and Mary Bard
State: Texas
Consultant: Karen Schmer
State: Colorado

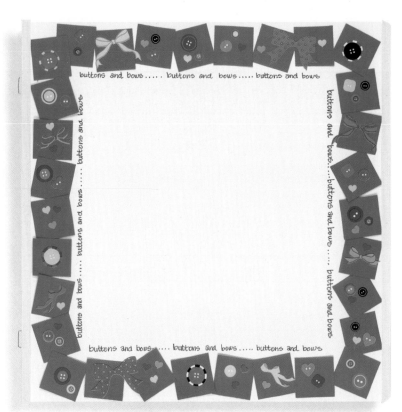

Materials:
- Multi Bow, Micro Heart & Button Stickers (Decorative Pack)
- Green Photo Mounting Paper (Contemporary Pack)
- Black Fine-Tip Pen

Special Instructions:
- Cut photo mounting paper into 1¼-inch squares

Consultant: Susan Coons
State: Georgia

ORDERS

Materials:
- Confetti, Balloon & Star Stickers (Creative Memories Introductory Pack)

Consultant: Joyce Rowell
State: Missouri

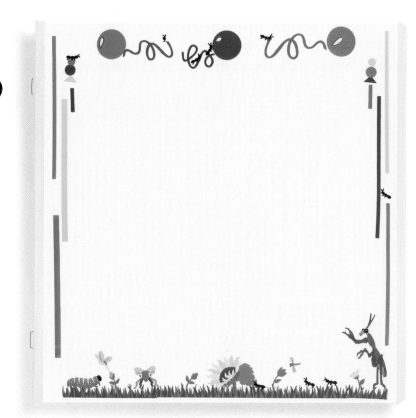

Materials:
- Confetti Stickers (Creative Memories Introductory Pack)
- Geometric Stickers (Big Pack)
- Insects, Grass, Sunflower & Micro Flower Stickers (Decorative Pack)

Special Instructions:
- Use the remaining parts of the confetti stickers on the circle stickers to make them look more like a balloon
- Use bottom sunflower from sunflower sticker

Consultant: Wilma Kardaseski
State: Colorado

ℬORDERS

Materials:
- Insect & Micro Flower Stickers (Decorative Pack)
- Die Cut Cactus & Sun
- Orange, Salmon, Lilac & Yellow Photo Mounting Paper (Contemporary Pack)
- Burgundy Photo Mounting Paper (Classic Pack)
- Circle Cutter
- Black Fine-Tip Pen

Consultant: Karen McAllister
State: California

Materials:
- Creative Memories Blue ABC Stickers
- Die Cut Miniature Fish
- Black Fine-Tip Pen

Consultant: Lisa M. Knott
State: California

CAMPING/FISHING

Materials:
- Creative Memories Red ABC Stickers
- Picnic, Camping & Fishing Stickers (Big Pack)
- Micro Stars (Decorative Pack)
- Die Cut Christmas Tree
- Deep Blue & Deep Blue Gingham Photo Mounting Paper
- Gold Photo Mounting Paper (Contemporary Pack)
- Brown Fine-Tip Pen
- Circle Cutter or Circle Template

Special Instructions:
- Create moon by cutting a circle out of gold photo mounting paper. Then cut half circle out of the original circle
- Cut stars off the Die Cut Christmas Trees. Cut one in half and mount halves on page edges

Consultant: Michelle Tachick
State: California

Materials:
- Bear Fishing Stickers (Big Pack)
- Die Cut Fish
- Arabesque Scissors
- Oval Template
- Blue & Black Fine-Tip Pens

Special Instructions:
- Cut a file folder with the Arabesque Scissors then trace for water line

Note: You can also use the Creative Memories Borderlines™ – *Wavy* or *Ocean* for a rough water option on this page

Consultant: Kathy Kittelson
State: Minnesota

CAMPING/FISHING

Materials:
- Camping & Fishing Stickers (Big Pack)
- Bear & Insect Stickers (Decorative Pack)
- Brown Photo Mounting Paper (Classic Pack)
- Evergreen, Evergreen Gingham & Cranberry Gingham Photo Mounting Paper
- Brown & Black Fine-Tip Pen
- Creative Memories Borderlines™ – *Wavy*

Special Instructions:
- Cut trees from Evergreen & Evergreen Gingham Photo Mounting Paper
- Cut handkerchief from Cranberry Gingham photo mounting paper

Consultant: Michelle Tachick
State: California

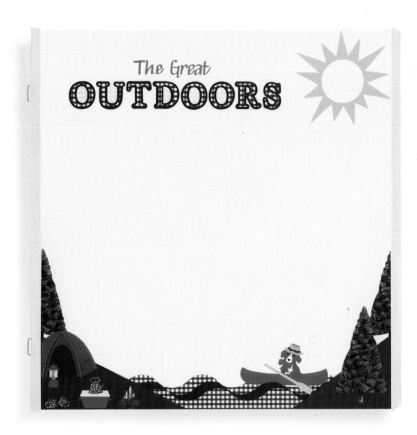

Materials:
- Camping & Pet Shop Stickers (Big Pack)
- Tree Stickers (Creative Memories Christmas Pack)
- Creative Memories Deep Blue ABC Sticker Stencils
- Deep Blue & Deep Blue Gingham Photo Mounting Paper
- Brown Photo Mounting Paper (Classic Pack)
- Die Cut Miniature Sun
- Red Calligraphy Pen
- Creative Memories Borderlines™ – *Wavy*

Special Instructions:
- Create letters using ABC sticker stencils and gingham paper. Cut around the letter stencils and pull from paper backing. Place randomly on gingham paper, including the center if the letter has one. With a straight-edge scissors, trim around colored frame. Mount letters with Creative Memories adhesive
- Note: To simplify, you may choose to use the Creative Memories ABC Stickers for your title

Consultant: Cindy Neal
State: California

CHILDREN

Materials:
- Creative Memories Black ABC/123 Stickers
- Micro Star Stickers (Decorative Pack)
- Die Cut Train
- Black Fine-Tip Pen

Consultant: Michelle Luke
State: Michigan

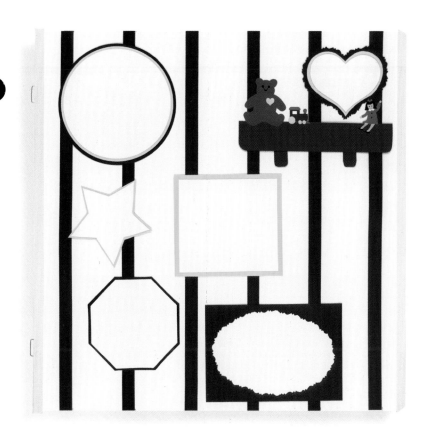

Materials:
- Toy Stickers, Bear & Micro Heart Stickers (Decorative Pack)
- Deep Blue & White Photo Mounting Paper
- Gold & Brown Photo Mounting Paper (Classic Pack)
- Star, Heart & Geometric Template
- Circle Cutter or Circle & Oval Template
- Alpine scissors

Special Instructions:
- Draw and cut out shelf from photo mounting paper

Note: The color scheme can be changed to create a girl's page

Consultant: Gregorita Lara
State: California

Materials:
- Playground Stickers (Big Pack)
- Die Cut Tricycle
- Red Fine-Tip Pen
- Blue Calligraphy Pen
- Creative Memories Borderlines™ – *Wavy*

Consultant: Michele Healy
State: Michigan

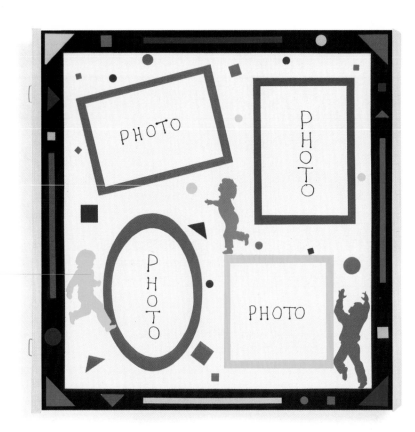

CHILDREN

Materials:
- Geometric & Dancing Children Stickers (Big Pack)
- Red, Gold, Green and Nautical Blue Photo Mounting Paper (Contemporary Pack)
- Black Photo Mounting Paper (Classic Pack)
- Oval Template

Consultant: Kimberly Arens
State: Nebraska

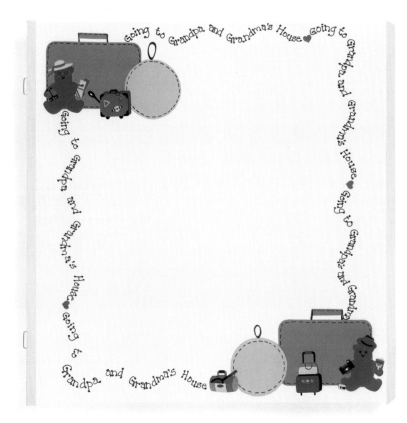

CHILDREN

Materials:
- Bear, Travel Gear Stickers & Micro Hearts (Decorative Pack)
- Light Pink & Sky Blue Photo Mounting Paper (Contemporary Pack)
- Black Fine-Tip Pen
- Creative Memories Borderlines™ – *Wavy*
- Circle Template or Circle Cutter
- Corner Rounder

Special Instructions:
- Use the wavy Borderlines™ as a guide for writing
- Use corner rounder on suitcase corners

Consultant: Kathy Kimes
State: Illinois

Materials:
- Micro Star & Super Star Stickers (Decorative Pack)
- Die Cut Clown
- Die Cut Letters
- Gold, Green & Nautical Blue Photo Mounting Paper (Contemporary Pack)
- White Photo Mounting Paper
- Scallop Scissors
- Black Calligraphy Pen
- Red & Blue Fine-Tip Pens
- Corner Rounder

Consultant: Michelle Luke
State: Michigan

CHILDREN

Materials:
- Gold Stars (Special Occasion Pack)
- Die Cut Angels
- Black Calligraphy Pen

Consultant: Janelle Peterson
State: Michigan

CHILDREN

Materials:
- Creative Memories Raspberry ABC Stickers
- Party Hat Stickers (Decorative Pack)
- Raspberry Photo Mounting Paper (Contemporary Pack)
- Navy Photo Mounting Paper (Classic Pack)
- Scallop Scissors

Special Instructions:
- Trace "pizza" with large circular object (e.g., a dinner plate)
- Cut raspberry paper with the "reverse" side of scallop scissors
- Mount circular photos randomly on "pizza"

Consultant: Robin Jansen
State: California

CHILDREN'S BIRTHDAY

Materials:
- Happy Birthday, Party & Confetti Stickers (Decorative Pack)
- Die Cut Clown
- Red, Gold, Green, Nautical Blue & Purple Photo Mounting Paper (Contemporary Pack)
- Black Fine-Tip Pen
- Circle Cutter or Circle Template

Special Instructions:
- Color part of the Clown's eye in with the black fine-tip pen
- Cut photo mounting paper and place behind clown for colored buttons

Consultant: Jossie L. Orense
State: California

CHILDREN'S BIRTHDAY

Materials:
- Happy Birthday, Micro Stars & Party Hat Stickers (Decorative Pack)
- Creative Memories Borderlines™ – *Victorian*
- Blue Calligraphy Pen

Consultant: Susanne Bodmer
State: New York

CHILDREN'S BIRTHDAY

Materials:
- Clown, Confetti, Happy Birthday, Toys, Party Hats, Multi Bow & Wagon Stickers (Decorative Pack)
- Red, Gold, Green, Nautical Blue & Black Photo Mounting Paper (Contemporary Pack)

Consultant: Jennifer C. Jones
State: Alabama

Materials:
- Micro Music Notes & Happy Birthday Stickers (Decorative Pack)
- Die Cut Ballerina/Slippers & Birthday Cake
- Pink Fine-Tip Pen
- Creative Memories Borderlines™ – *Wavy*

Special Instructions:
- Cut Candles off of the die cut birthday cake

Consultant: Sandra L. Stapleton
State: Ohio

FALL

Materials:
- Creative Memories Cranberry & Evergreen ABC Stickers
- Autumn Border, Small Leaves & Pumpkin Stickers (Special Occasion Pack)
- Cranberry & Evergreen Photo Mounting Paper
- Orange & Green Fine-Tip Pen
- Creative Memories Borderlines™ – *Wavy*

Combined Ideas From:
Consultant: Lynn Hyche
State: Alabama
Consultant: Lorraine Paffenroth
State: Michigan

Materials:
- Small Leaves Stickers (Special Occasion Pack)
- Die Cut Oak Leaves & Acorns
- Brown Photo Mounting Paper (Classic Pack)
- Evergreen Photo Mounting Paper
- Deckle Trimmer or Alpine Scissors

Consultant: Karen McAllister
State: California

ℱALL

Materials:
- Grass Stickers (Decorative Pack)
- Pumpkin & Autumn Border Stickers (Special Occasion Pack)
- Die Cut Scarecrow & Pumpkin
- Evergreen Gingham Photo Mounting Paper
- Green Calligraphy Pen
- Creative Memories Borderlines™ – *Wavy*

Consultant: Carmen Frey
State: California

41

WOLK 1920

Charles baking bread.

Charles and Elizabeth are in front.

Cornelia Mundy (Elizabeth's sister) Charles Wolk and Elizabeth, his wife.

Charles Wolk was the Brew Meister at Anheuser-Busch in St. Louis before prohibition. When the brewery closed, he started his own bakery at 4173 Gasconade Ave.

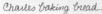
The Charles Wolk Bakery, St. Louis., Mo.

Materials:
- Creative Memories Black ABC/123 Stickers
- Heart Stickers (Creative Memories Wedding Pack)
- Black Photo Mounting Paper (Contemporary Pack)
- Brown & Black Fine-Tip Pens

Special Instructions:
- Cut through large hearts to weave together

Consultant: Melynna Wolk
State: Missouri

Materials:
- Charcoal, Black & Burgundy Photo Mounting Paper (Classic Pack)
- Deckle Trimmer or Alpine Scissors

Consultant: Juli Shulem
State: California

Materials:
- Rose with Ribbon Sticker (Special Occasion Pack)
- Dusty Rose & Light Blue Photo Mounting Paper (Classic Pack)
- White Photo Mounting Paper
- Arabesque Scissors
- Corner Rounder

Consultant: Debbie Siwy
Province: Alberta

Materials:
- Charcoal Photo Mounting Paper (Neutral Pack)
- Creative Memories Borderlines™ – *Victorian*
- Arabesque Scissors
- Circle Cutter
- Oval Template
- Brown Fine-Tip Pen

Consultants: Kendra Yoder, Cindy Yoder & Susie Lee
State: Indiana

Materials:
- Creative Memories Raspberry ABC Stickers
- Grass, Micro Hearts & Multi Bow Stickers (Decorative Pack)
- Pet Shop Stickers (Big Pack)
- Die Cut Heart & Paw Print
- Black Fine-Tip Pen

Consultant: Judy Bailey
State: Texas

Materials:
- Pet Shop Stickers (Big Pack)
- Die Cut Paw Print
- Die Cut Letters
- Black Fine-Tip Pen

Consultant: Leah Jane Jeppson
State: Utah

Materials:
- Pet Shop Stickers (Big Pack)
- Top Hat with Rose Stickers (Special Occasion Pack)
- Grass Stickers (Decorative Pack)
- Red Photo Mounting Paper (Contemporary Pack)
- Brown & Black Fine-Tip Pens
- Creative Memories Borderlines™ – *Wavy*
- Die Cut Paw Print

Special Instructions:
- Use "toes" from die cut paw print to create smaller paw prints

Consultant: Jody Price
State: Michigan

$\mathcal{S}$CHOOL

Materials:
- Creative Memories Green ABC/123 Stickers
- Vehicle Stickers (Big Pack)
- Die Cut School House, Apple & Miniature Apples
- Red Photo Mounting Paper (Contemporary Pack)
- Green Fine-Tip & Calligraphy Pens
- Corner Rounder

Consultant: Belinda Nasholm
State: Oregon

Materials:
- Grass & Micro Music Note Stickers (Decorative Pack)
- Playground Stickers (Big Pack)
- Die Cut Miniature Apples
- Black & Green Fine-Tip Pens
- Creative Memories Borderlines™ – *Wavy*

Consultant: Linda Miller
State: Georgia

Games...Duck-Duck Goose, Jumprope, Hopscotch, Kitty in the Corner

My First Grade Class at Cornucopia School 1958-59

CORNUCOPIA SCHOOL - GRADES 1 & 2 - 1958-59

Record the names of students here.

Journal memories in a narrative here. Include the name of your teacher, the number of students in your class, how you got to school – walked, rode the bus..., and other interesting comments about your school year.

School Memories....Fun with Dick and Jane.... See Spot run. See Puff. Go, go, go.

Songs... Good Morning to You, Sing Your Way Home

Best Friends... Diana, Diane, Carol

SCHOOL

Materials:
- Small Apple & Ivy Stickers (Decorative Pack)
- Red Photo Mounting Paper (Contemporary Pack)
- White Photo Mounting Paper
- Red & Black Fine-Tip Pens

Consultant: Nancy Mintz
State: Montana

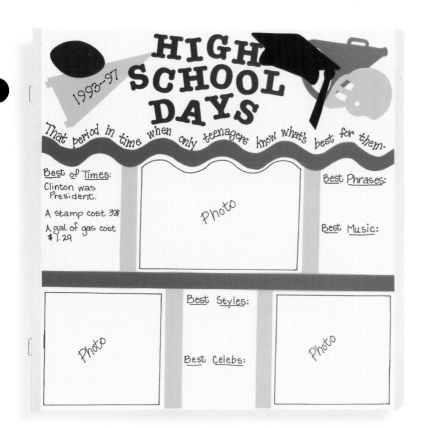

Materials:
- Creative Memories Blue ABC Stickers
- Die Cut Football, Team Pennants, Megaphone, Football Helmet & Graduation Hat
- Gold & Red Photo Mounting Paper (Classic Pack)
- Black Fine-Tip Pen
- Creative Memories Borderlines™ – *Wavy*

Consultant: Julie Shafii
State: California

Materials:
- Books, Pen & Crayon, Micro Stars & Super Star Stickers (Decorative Pack)
- Die Cut Oval Frame & Miniature Apple
- Red, Gold & Purple Photo Mounting Paper (Contemporary Pack)

Special Instructions:
- Draw and cut books out of photo mounting paper

Consultant: Nancy Mintz
State: Montana

Materials:
- Party, Book, Super Star & Grass Stickers (Decorative Pack)
- Graduation Stickers (Special Occasion Pack)
- Camera & Dancing Children Stickers (Big Pack)
- Die Cut Graduation Hat
- Black Photo Mounting Paper (Contemporary Pack)
- White Photo Mounting Paper
- Black Fine-Tip Pen
- Yellow Sumi Brush Pen

Consultant: Michelle Tachick
State: California

CHOOL

Materials:
- Creative Memories Black ABC Stickers
- Small Rose, Micro Stars & Music Notes (Decorative Pack)
- Cinnamon Hearts (Special Occasion Pack)
- Black Fine-Tip & Calligraphy Pens
- Creative Memories Borderlines™ – *Wavy*

Consultant: Cindy Neal
State: California

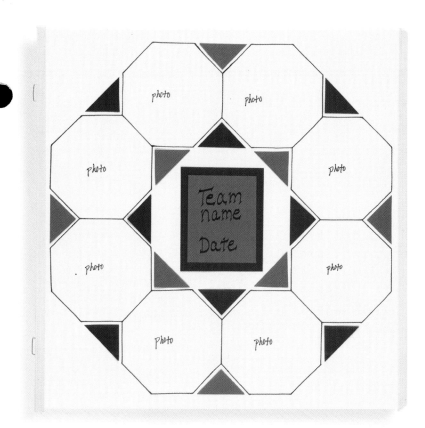

Materials:
- Purple & Navy Blue Photo Mounting Paper (Classic Pack)
- Geometric Template
- Black Calligraphy Pen

Note: The color scheme can be changed to appropriate team colors

Consultant: Angie Poynter
State: California

PORTS

Materials:
- Creative Memories Gold ABC Stickers
- Die Cut Star & Trophy
- Red & Nautical Blue Photo Mounting Paper (Contemporary Pack)
- Red Fine-Tip Pen

Consultant: Kimberly Spurlock
State: Texas

Materials:
- Creative Memories Red ABC Stickers
- Confetti & Star Stickers (Creative Memories Introductory Pack)
- Red, Gold & Nautical Blue Photo Mounting Paper (Contemporary Pack)
- Light Blue Photo Mounting Paper (Classic Pack)
- Deep Blue Photo Mounting Paper
- Black Fine-Tip Pen
- Circle Cutter or Circle Template
- Star Template
- Corner Rounder

Special Instructions:
- Draw volleyball and net with fine-tip pen

Note: Deep Blue Gingham photo mounting paper can be used for the volleyball net

Consultant: Kymm Schultz
State: Arizona

SPORTS

Materials:
- Creative Memories Red ABC/123 Stickers
- Die Cut Bat, Ball, Glove, Tennis Racket, Team Pennant, Football, Sunglasses, Graduation Hat, Megaphone, Football Helmet & Star
- Deep Blue Gingham Photo Mounting Paper
- Blue & Black Fine-Tip Pens

Consultant: Cindy Neal
State: California

Materials:
- Creative Memories Raspberry ABC Stickers
- Grass Stickers (Decorative Pack)
- Raspberry, Pink, Purple & Green Photo Mounting Paper (Contemporary Pack)
- Evergreen Gingham Photo Mounting Paper
- Alpine Scissors
- Oval Template

Special Instructions:
- Cut one oval with the Alpine Scissors and one with a straight-edge scissors
- Cut the smooth edge in half using Alpine Scissors
- Draw and cut petals from evergreen gingham paper

Consultant: Donna Sherman
State: Washington

Materials:
- Creative Memories Gold & Green ABC/123 Stickers
- Grass & Insect Stickers (Decorative Pack)
- Die Cut Sunflower & Flower Pot
- Gold Photo Mounting Paper (Contemporary Pack)
- Brown Photo Mounting Paper (Classic Pack)
- Black Fine-Tip Pen

Special Instructions:
- Place brown photo mounting paper behind center of sunflower die cut shape
- Overlap Gold and Green ABC/123 Stickers

Consultant: Traci Goshen and Customer Julie Johnson
State: California

PRING

Materials:
- Creative Memories Raspberry & Sky Blue ABC Stickers
- Travel Gear & Palm Tree Stickers (Decorative Pack)
- Die Cut Film Frame
- Cream Photo Mounting Paper (Classic Pack)

Special Instructions:
- Alternate and overlap Raspberry and Sky Blue ABC Stickers

Consultant: Roshele Snyder
State: California

SUMMER

Materials:
- Die Cut Sun with Stencil, Film Frame with inside and outside Stencil & Sunglasses
- Oval Template

Consultant: Barbara Sakakihara
State: California

Materials:
- Insect Stickers (Decorative Pack)
- Red & Green Photo Mounting Paper (Contemporary Pack)
- Cranberry Gingham Photo Mounting Paper
- Red, Green & Black Fine-Tip Pens

Consultant: Lynnette Adams
State: Washington

UMMER

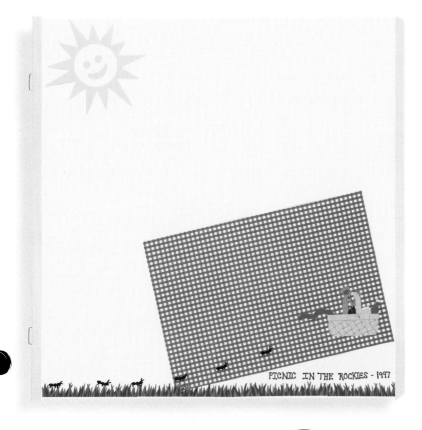

Materials:
- Insect & Grass Stickers (Decorative Pack)
- Basket Stickers (Special Occasion Pack)
- Picnic Stickers (Big Pack)
- Die Cut Miniature Sun
- Cranberry Gingham Photo Mounting Paper
- Black Fine-Tip Pen

Consultant: Terrie Westlake
State: Colorado

Materials:
- Creative Memories Black & Gold ABC Stickers
- Bear Stickers (Decorative Pack)
- Beach Stickers (Big Pack)

Special Instructions:
- Overlap Black and Gold ABC Stickers

Consultant: Jean Fennema
State: Illinois

SUMMER

Materials:
- Creative Memories Black ABC Stickers
- Micro Flower Stickers (Decorative Pack)
- Die Cut Horse
- Green Photo Mounting Paper (Contemporary Pack)
- Evergreen Photo Mounting Paper

Special Instructions:
- Tear photo mounting paper to create the "rough" edge

Consultant: Lori L. Ruskamp
State: Nebraska

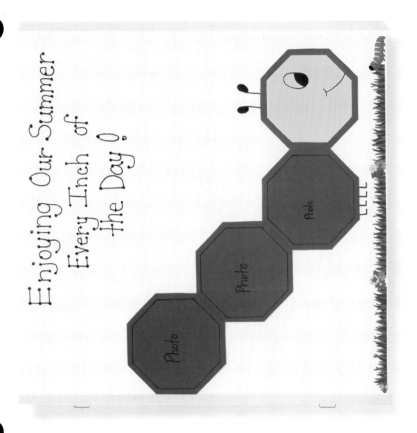

Enjoying Our Summer
Every Inch of
the Day !

Consultant: Lori Stevens
State: Mississippi

Materials:
- Micro Flowers, Grass & Insect Stickers (Decorative Pack)
- Die Cut Sun
- Green & Gold Photo Mounting Paper (Classic Pack)
- Geometric Template
- Black Fine-Tip Pen

DOUBLE PAGE SPREAD

SUMMER

Materials:
- Playground Stickers (Big Pack)
- Die Cut Sun
- Die Cut Letters

Consultant: Lisa Stienstra
State: California

VACATION

Materials:
- Creative Memories Lilac ABC Stickers
- Large Animal Stickers (Big Pack)
- Travel Gear Stickers (Decorative Pack)
- Black Fine-Tip Pen

Special Instructions:
- Use black fine-tip pen to create camera strap around the giraffe's neck

Consultant: Char Mulligan-Micek
State: Colorado

Materials:
- Creative Memories Black ABC/123 Stickers
- Travel Gear Stickers (Decorative Pack)
- Teal Photo Mounting Paper (Contemporary Pack)
- Navy Blue & Red Photo Mounting Paper (Classic Pack)
- Creative Memories Borderlines™ – *Scallop*

Special Instructions:
- Trace scallop Borderlines™ to create circles

Consultant: Jossie L. Orense
State: California

Vacation

Materials:
- Creative Memories Blue ABC Stickers
- Teal & Sky Blue Photo Mounting Paper (Contemporary Paper)
- Palm Tree & Travel Gear Stickers (Decorative Pack)
- Die Cut Dolphin & Stencil
- Blue & Green Fine-Tip Pens
- Geometric Template
- Alpine Scissors
- Creative Memories Borderlines™ – *Victorian*

Special Instructions:
- Cut around die cut shape stencil with straight-edge scissors to make dolphin

Consultant: Mary K. O'Brien
State: California

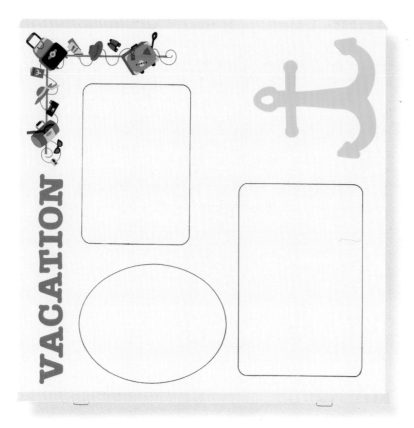

Consultant: Michelle S. Rose
State: Texas

Materials:
- Creative Memories Raspberry ABC Stickers
- Travel Gear Stickers (Decorative Pack)
- Die Cut Airplane & Anchor
- Green Calligraphy Pen
- Pink Fine-Tip Pen
- Circle & Oval Template
- Corner Rounder

*D*OUBLE PAGE SPREAD

Materials:
- Creative Memories Hot Pink ABC/123 Stickers
- Confetti, Flower & Heart Stickers (Creative Memories Wedding Pack)
- Die Cut Wedding Bells

Consultant: Laurie Grover
State: Minnesota

WEDDING/ANNIVERSARY

Materials:
- Wedding Stickers (Creative Memories Wedding Pack)
- Creative Memories Borderlines™ – *Wavy*
- Pink Fine-Tip & Calligraphy Pens

Consultant: Luana Bastien
State: California

Shower

Materials:
- Wedding Stickers (Creative Memories Wedding Pack)
- Pink Fine-Tip Pen
- Creative Memories Borderlines™ – *Wavy*
- Oval Template

Special Instructions:
- Cut photos with oval template

Consultant: Janet Distelzweig
State: Michigan

LOVE

OF THESE IS ... BUT THE GREATEST ... LOVE NEVER FAILS... ALWAYS PERSEVERES ALWAYS HOPES ALWAYS TRUSTS ALWAYS PROTECTS IT ALWAYS

LOVE IS PATIENT LOVE IS KIND IT DOES NOT ENVY IT DOES NOT BOAST IT IS NOT PROUD IT IS NOT RUDE IT IS NOT SELF-SEEKING

IT IS NOT EASILY ANGERED IT KEEPS NO RECORD OF WRONGS LOVE DOES NOT DELIGHT IN EVIL BUT REJOICES WITH THE TRUTH

Photo of Groom

Photo of Bride

Photo of Wedding Party

WEDDING/ANNIVERSARY

Materials:
- Heart & Bouquet Stickers (Creative Memories Wedding Pack)
- Deep Blue Photo Mounting Paper
- Die Cut Letter Stencils
- Black Fine-Tip Pen
- Creative Memories Borderlines™ – *Victorian*
- Alpine Scissors
- Corner Rounder

Special Instructions:
- Trace die cut stencils on deep blue paper. Cut out with Alpine Scissors
- Trim the corners of photos with the Alpine Scissors
- Use Victorian Borderline as a guide when writing the border

Consultant: Jennifer Surra-Dayley
State: Idaho

Materials:
- Die Cut Skier, Miniature Sun & Christmas Tree
- Sky Blue Photo Mounting Paper (Contemporary Pack)
- Deep Blue Photo Mounting Paper

Special Instructions:
- Cut off star from Christmas tree die cut shape

Consultant: Carol Wang
Province: Alberta

WINTER

Materials:
- Creative Memories Light Blue ABC Stickers
- Die Cut Snowman & Miniature Snowflakes
- Black, Orange & Nautical Blue Photo Mounting Paper (Contemporary Pack)
- Blue Fine-Tip Pen

Special Instructions:
- Place black and orange photo mounting paper behind snowman face
- Trace outline of hat with blue fine-tip pen

Consultant: Kathy J. Watson
State: Michigan

Materials:
- Creative Memories Blue ABC Stickers
- Snowflake Stickers (Creative Memories Christmas Pack)
- Die Cut Snowflake
- Creative Memories Borderlines™ – *Wavy*
- Blue Fine-Tip & Calligraphy Pens

Consultant: Kathy J. Watson
State: Michigan

𝒲INTER

Materials:
- Creative Memories Black ABC/123 Stickers
- Snow Tree Stickers (Special Occasion Pack)
- Evergreen Photo Mounting Paper
- Red Photo Mounting Paper (Contemporary Pack)
- Black Calligraphy Pen

Special Instructions:
- Draw & cut sled from photo mounting paper

Consultant: Carmen Whisonant
State: North Dakota

Materials:
- Creative Memories Black ABC Stickers
- Camera Stickers (Big Pack)
- Black Photo Mounting Paper (Contemporary Pack)
- Black Calligraphy Pen

Consultant: Shelley Dodson
State: Arizona

MISCELLANEOUS

Materials:
- Red Photo Mounting Paper (Contemporary Pack)
- Die Cut Letter Stencils
- Black Fine-Tip Pen
- Scallop Scissors
- Oval Template

Special Instructions:
- Cut edges off stencils with Scallop scissors. Adhere clippings around the edge of the page
- Draw & cut "blasts" from photo mounting paper

Consultant: Patricia Anderson
State: Arizona

Materials:
- Micro Flower Stickers (Decorative Pack)
- Ivy Stickers (Special Occasion Pack)
- Die Cut Church & Cathedral Window
- Yellow & Purple Photo Mounting Paper (Contemporary Pack)
- Purple Fine-Tip Pen
- Creative Memories Borderlines™ – *Wavy*
- Scallop Scissors
- Circle Cutter
- Oval Template
- Corner Rounder

Consultant: Mary K. O'Brien
State: California

MISCELLANEOUS

Materials:
- Evergreen & Evergreen Gingham Photo Mounting Paper
- Brown Photo Mounting Paper (Classic Pack)
- Alpine Scissors

Consultant: Patti Bechtold
State: Colorado
Designed by
Customer Jackie Desrosiers

Materials:
- Micro Heart, Micro Flower & Insect Stickers (Decorative Pack)
- Pet Shop & Sea Creature Stickers (Big Pack)
- Pink Calligraphy Pen
- Green Fine-Tip Pen
- Creative Memories Borderlines™ – *Victorian*

Consultant: Donna Sherman
State: Washington

Materials:
- Creative Memories Red ABC Stickers
- Confetti Stickers (Creative Memories Introductory Pack)
- Die Cut Megaphone & Maple Leaves

Consultant: Diane Major
Province: British Columbia

BABY

Hush little baby

Rock-a-bye baby

The apple of our eye

We never know the love of a parent until we become parents ourselves – *Henry Ward Beecher*

Cleaning and scrubbing
   can wait 'til tomorrow
For babies grow up
   we've learned to our sorrow
So quiet down cobwebs,
   dust go to sleep
I'm rocking my baby
   and babies don't keep!
– *Hamilton*

May you always walk in sunshine, may your wildest dreams come true!
– *Unknown*

Good night, sweetheart,
Good night – *McGuire Sisters*

Little bitty pretty one

I begin to love this little creature, and to anticipate (her) birth as a fresh twist to a knot, which I do not wish to untie.
– *Mary Wollstonecraft*

Who is getting more pleasure from this rocking, the baby or me?
– *Nancy Thayer*

BIRTHDAY

There's no time like the presents! – *Mary Engelbreit*

Happy Birthday to you!

But now I am six,
I'm as clever as clever
So I think I'll be six
now for ever and ever!!!
– *A. A. Milne*

CHILDREN

You are my sunshine

My brother, my best friend!

What are little girls made of? Sugar and spice and everything nice. – *Mother Goose*

Rub-a-dub-dub
There's a boy (girl) in the tub
Splashing and shouting with glee.
She's scrubbed and (s)he's rubbed
and (s)he's played in the tub
and now (s)he's as clean as can be.
– *C. Mahmood,*
adapted from Mother Goose

We have been friends together in sunshine and in shade.
– *Caroline Norton*

Girls just wanna have fun

What feeling is so nice as a child's hand in yours? So small, so soft and warm, like a kitten huddling in the shelter of your clasp.
– *Marjorie Holmes*

It will be gone before you know it. The fingerprints on the wall appear higher and higher. Then suddenly they disappear. – *Dorothy Evslin*

Teenagers are people who express a burning desire to be different by dressing exactly alike. – *Anonymous*

DANCING

You make me feel
like dancing – *Bee Gees*

Rock around the clock
– *Bill Haley & The Comets*

Let's sing! Let's eat! Let's jiggle our feet! – *Mary Engelbreit*

Boot scootin' boogie
– *Brooks & Dunn*

GRADUATION

These happy days are yours and mine – *Norman Gimbel*

And when you have reached the mountain top, then you shall begin to climb – *Kahlil Gibran*

I am not afraid of storms for I am learning how to sail my ship – *Louisa May Alcott*

Still round the corner there may wait, a new road or a secret gate – *J.R.R. Tolkien*

Climb every mountain
search every stream
follow every rainbow
'til you find your dream
– *Rogers and Hammerstein*

Two roads diverged in a wood, and I took the one less traveled by, And that has made all the difference – *Robert Frost*

MISCELLANEOUS

For everything there is a season, and a time for every purpose under the heaven. – *Ecclesiates*

If my friends could
see me now! – *Dorothy Fields*

A piece of cake!

It is not how much we have, but how much we enjoy, that makes happiness. – *C.H. Spurgeon*

Let me be aware
of the treasure you are!

The ornaments of our house are the friends that frequent it
– *Emerson*

You can never
have too many friends

The trick is to live a long time without growing old – *Unknown*

The one absolutely unselfish
friend that man can have in this
selfish world is his dog.
– *Unknown*

How much is that doggy
in the window?
The one with the waggley tail.
I do hope that doggy's for sale!
– *Unknown*

All things bright and beautiful
All creatures great and small,
All things wise and wonderful,
The Lord God made them all.
– *Cecil Alexander*

Me and my shadow.
– *Billy Rose*

I like to walk about amidst the
beautiful things that adorn the
world – *Eugene Field*

You must do the thing you think
you cannot do. – *Eleanor Roosevelt*

Mid pleasures and palaces through
we may roam, be it ever so
humble, there's no place like
home. – *John Howard Payne*

SCHOOL

The wheels on the bus
go 'round and 'round

School days, school days,
good old golden rule days!

SPORTS

Take me out to the ball game
Buy me some peanuts and
crackerjacks – *Jack Norworth*

It ain't over 'til it's over
– *Casey Stengle*

Win one for the gipper
– *Knute Rockney*

SPRING

Singing in the rain,
just singing in the rain
– *Arthur Freed*

Spring has sprung!

Though April showers may come
your way, they bring the flowers
that bloom in May.
– *Unknown*

O laugh and sing, Give welcome
to the Spring! – *M. Livingston*

Float like a butterfly,
sting like a bee. – *Muhammad Ali*

SUMMER

It's like a heatwave!

Those lazy hazy days of Summer
– *Nat King Cole*

Fun in the sun!

Under the sea, just you and me.
Baby it's better, down where it's
wetter. Take it from me.
– *Flounder, in the Little Mermaid*

One fish, two fish,
red fish, blue fish. – *Dr. Seuss*

Walkin' on sunshine
– *Katrina & The Waves*

FALL

Autumn scuffs across the earth,
leaves it patched and brown,
holds his cap to catch the acorns
falling to the ground.
Autumn leaves a fringe of frost
when pumpkins turn to gold,
pulls his collar up to warm his face
grown gray and old
Autumn calls the winning toss,
passes for a gain,
blocks the frost with bittersweet,
takes the pouring rain.
– *Unknown*

WINTER

Let it snow, let it snow, let it snow!

Walkin' in a winter wonderland

Spinning icicles of glass!

Snowflakes and little boys.
There are no two alike.

TITLE PAGE

I lay this book in your lap.
Say you are surprised?
Say you liked it?
Say it's just what you wanted?
Because it's yours…
Because I love you…
– *from Winnie the Pooh,
A.A. Milne*

FOR A CHILD'S ALBUM:

You may have
tangible wealth untold
Caskets of jewels and
coffers of gold.
Richer than I can ever be,
I have a mother who made a
scrapbook for me!
– *Adapted from the Reading
Mother by Strickland Gillian*

VACATION

Just another day in paradise

On the road again – *Willie Nelson*

I must go down to the sea again

By the sea, by the sea,
by the beautiful sea.
You and me, you and me,
oh how happy we will be.
– *Unknown*

WEDDING/LOVE

When I fall in love,
it will be forever.
When I give my heart,
it will be completely.
– *Edward Heyman*

Oh how we danced on the night
we were wed – *Al Johnson*

I'll be loving you always

We've only just begun
– *Karen Carpenter*

Love will keep us together
– *Captain & Tennille*

One love that is shared by two
– *Streisand*

A kiss for luck and we're on our way – *Paul Williams*

Love is patient, love is kind, it does not boast. It is not proud, it is not rude; it is not self-seeking, it is not easily angered, it keeps no record of wrongs. Love does not delight in evil but rejoices with the truth. It always protects, always trusts, always hopes, always preserves. Love never fails...but the greatest of these is Love.
– *I Corinthians 13:4-8, 13*

To love a person means to agree to grow old with him. – *Albert Camus*

The days of wine and roses – *Mancini*

My funny Valentine – *Lorenz Hart*

It had to be you! – *Gus Kahn*

A time for us – *Kusik, Snyder*

How sweet it is to be loved by you – *Eddie Holland*

Love makes the world go 'round – *Bob Merrill*

A woman who has never seen her husband fishing doesn't know what a patient man she married!
– *Unknown*

Love is not a matter of counting the years, it's making the years count. – *William Smith*

How do I love thee? Let me count the ways.
– *Elizabeth Barrett Browning*

If ever two were one, then surely we. If ever man were loved by wife, then thee. – *Anne Bradstreet*

NEW YEAR

Fast away the old year passes – *Welsh Carol*

MOTHER'S DAY & FATHER'S DAY

Anyone can be a father, but it takes someone special to be a daddy.

Who ran to help me when I fell and would some pretty story tell Or kiss the place to make it well My Mother – *Ann Taylor*

Nobody knows of the work it takes to keep the home together, Nobody knows of the steps it takes, nobody knows – but Mother.
– *Anonymous*

Dear Mother: I'm all right. Stop worrying about me.
– *Egyptian Papyrus Letter*

FOR PHOTOS WITH DAD:

Hop Pop We like to hop We like to hop on top of Pop!
– *Dr. Seuss*

GRANDMOTHER'S

Grandma was a kind of first-aid station, or a Red Cross nurse, who took up where the battle ended, accepting us and our little sobbing sins, gathering the whole of us into her lap, restoring us to health and confidence by her amazing faith in life and in a mortal's strength to meet it.
– *Lillian Smith*

FAMILY

The family – that dear octopus from whose tentacles we never quite escape, nor, in our inmost hearts, ever quite wish to.
– *Dodie Smith*

CHRISTMAS

Never a Christmas morning Never an old year ends but someone thinks of someone Old days old times old friends.
– *Unknown*

Santa Claus is coming to town – *Louie Armstrong*

All I want for Christmas is my two front teeth – *Tony Bennett*

All is calm, all is bright – *Franz Gruber*

Dashing through the snow – *James Pierpont*

Silent night, Holy night

Deck the halls – *Welsh Carol*

Peace on earth, goodwill to men – *Edmund Sears*

Good friends are a special treat!

The best Christmas gift of all is the presence of a happy family all wrapped up with one another.
– *Unknown*

I'm dreaming of a white Christmas Just like the ones I used to know, Where the treetops glisten And the children listen To hear sleigh bells in the snow.
– *Irving Berlin*

Every effort has been made to locate the copyright holders of materials used in this book. Should there be any omissions or errors, we apologize and shall be pleased to make the appropriate acknowledgements in future editions.

Thanks to Creative Memories Consultants who submitted this "at a loss for words" concept.
Consultants: Chris Peters, Carrin Mahmood, Janelle Dickinson, Denise Oie, Robin Anderson, Laurie Englund, Kathy Povolny
State: Minnesota